W9-AYO-128

Eck

Sports

I Can Ski

By Edana Eckart

Welcome Books™

Children's Press®
A Division of Scholastic Inc.
New York / Toronto / London / Auckland / Sydney
Mexico City / New Delhi / Hong Kong
Danbury, Connecticut

Thanks to the Chill program. Chill is a non-profit learn-to-snowboard program for disadvantaged inner-city kids. For more information on this national intervention program, please contact jennd@burton.com.
Thanks to Rossignol

Photo Credits: Cover and all photos by Maura B. McConnell
Contributing Editor: Jennifer Silate
Book Design: Mindy Liu

Library of Congress Cataloging-in-Publication Data

Eckart, Edana.
  I can ski / by Edana Eckart.
  p. cm. — (Sports)
  Summary: When a young girl and her father go skiing, she shows how to ski properly and safely.
  Includes bibliographical references (p.   ) and index.
  ISBN 0-516-24277-6 (lib. bdg.) — ISBN 0-516-24369-1 (pbk.)
  1. Skis and skiing—Juvenile literature. [1. Skis and skiing.] I. Title.

GV854.315 .E34 2003
796.93—dc21

2002007071

Contents

My name is Leslie.

Today, I am going to **ski**.

5

I wear **goggles** to ski.

They will keep snow and wind out of my eyes.

I also put on warm clothes to ski.

I wear a scarf, a coat, and gloves.

9

I wear special **boots** to ski, too.

Each boot fits onto a ski.

The boots will stay on the skis.

Mom and I will ride the **lift** to the top of the hill.

We will ski down the hill.

13

Now, it is time to ski.

I push with my ski
to go forward.

15

I want to turn left.

I **lean** on my left ski to turn.

17

I ski down the hill.

I am **careful** not to fall.

Mom skis with me.

19

I made it to the bottom of the hill.

I point my skis together to stop.

Skiing is fun!

21

New Words

boots (**boots**) heavy shoes that cover your ankles and sometimes part of your leg

careful (**kair**-fuhl) to pay close attention when doing something

goggles (**gog**-uhlz) special glasses that fit tightly around your eyes to protect them

lean (**leen**) to bend toward or over something

lift (**lift**) a machine that takes people to the top of a mountain or hill

ski (**skee**) a pair of long, narrow pieces of wood or other material that are fastened to boots; moving over snow on skis

To Find Out More

Books
Skiing
by Larry Dane Brimner
Children's Press

Snow Skiing
by Tracy Maurer
The Rourke Book Company

Web Site
Telluride Kids
http://www.telluridekids.com/
Learn about skiing and play fun games on this Web site.

Index

About the Author
Edana Eckart has written several children's books. She enjoys bike riding with her family.

Reading Consultants
Kris Flynn, Coordinator, Small School District Literacy, The San Diego County Office of Education

Shelly Forys, Certified Reading Recovery Specialist, W.J. Zahnow Elementary School, Waterloo, IL

Sue McAdams, Former President of the North Texas Reading Council of the IRA, and Early Literacy Consultant, Dallas, TX